Contents (Second

C000177078

The East Berkshire RA Group was formed in 1970 to protect and restore to good order all the public rights of way in this part of Berkshire, and also to seek improvements to the existing footpath network. The Group endeavours to keep under regular surveillance all 1200 paths in the area and will take up irregularities with parish councils, district councils and the County Council to preserve public rights.

Working parties of Group members have cleared over 48 miles of overgrown paths, erected or repaired 605 signposts, built or repaired 220 stiles and 86 footbridges. Regular walks are held, to which newcomers are always welcome, to encourage the use of paths and enjoyment of the countryside. For further details of the Group please contact the Membership Secretary:

Rita North, Rosette Cottage, High Street, Hurley, Nr. Maidenhead, Berkshire SL6 5LT.

Maps in this book are based upon the Ordnance Survey map with the sanction of the Controller of HM Stationery Office. Crown copyright reserved.

Mount Hill and Malders Lane

This circular walk, of about 3 miles in length, is through the farmland and woodland between Maidenhead and Cookham Dean. The early and latter stages of this walk are across parts of the Maidenhead and Cookham Commons (total 848 acres), which with the Lordship of the Manor, were acquired for £2,800 by public subscription in 1934 and handed over to the National Trust to be managed by a Local Preservation Committee.

The directions below start from the Cookham Dean Common National Trust car park in Winter Hill Road (Grid Ref. 862843), but the map of the route may suggest other starting places. The map also shows a slightly shorter walk via Mount Farm and Beeching Grove Wood. For further topographical features of the area, see the Ordnance Survey 1:25,000 'Pathfinder' series map Sheet1157 'Maidenhead and Marlow'. Please observe the Country Code; in particular, keep to footpaths, keep dogs on lead across farmland and leave all wild flowers for others to enjoy.

With your back to the road, follow path from National Trust sign, to shortly turn left to follow edge of common. Some 50 yards before garden of large house ahead ('Coombe End'), turn right still keeping to edge of common with woodland on left. 30 yards before reaching far corner, turn left into narrow path through woodland strip to shortly reach metalled road. Continue straight on along road, keep right at the small Bigfrith Green (NT), then after about 30 yards along road, fork right across grass to enter hedged path between properties 'Printers Pie' and 'Darbys'. Pass through horse-barrier and climb slowly through left and right-hand bends to reach gravel track, Pudseys Close, then continue ahead to reach road – Spring Lane. Here look to the right for the summit of – Mount Hill.

With care turn right down the narrow winding lane and observe through gaps in fence and hedge on left – Bourne End

and Cookham in Thames Valley below, and Cliveden House (NT) more distant in the woods above. Where road forks at letterbox, continue left along Spring Lane and shortly cross over road (Long Lane) to enter well-defined path through middle of field. Here pause awhile for views of Maidenhead and distant Windsor Castle to the left. At end of first field, with clump of trees to left, continue ahead, down gently sloping track with fence on left to reach bend in metalled road next to buildings of Cannon Court Farm, here turn right along gravel track - Malders Lane.

Near top of rise, at near corner of cottage 'Cannonwood' on left, look right on top of bank next to fence for a 1934 Maidenhead Borough boundary stone – one of the thirty stones still to be found around the old Maidenhead Borough boundary. Continue along Malders lane, passing row of white painted 1879 cottages on left, then at end of first building (on left) at Hindhay Farm, turn right over stile and along edge of field with fence on left.

About half-way along field, fork left into woodland path with fence on left, then at shed in corner of property (Heron's Court) on left, turn right to follow waymarked (painted white arrows) woodland path to reach road junction at 'Butlers Gate' cottage. Opposite end of cottage notice another boundary stone on roadside bank. At road junction, turn right in to Choke Lane and then immediately fork left into broad woodland path on Cookham Dean Common (NT). Emerging from woodland, turn sharp left and then eventually right, to follow ride around perimeter of common to return to car park at start.

Footnote: for details of the Maidenhead Boundary Walk, the historic Beating the Bounds ceremony and the location of all the boundary stones, see the companion booklet 'Beating the Bounds Around Maidenhead'.

DATE WALKED

		19

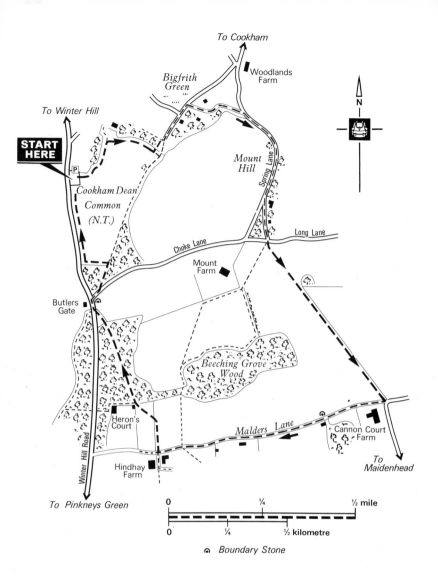

To Cookham

Woodlands Farm

Bigfrith Green

To Winter Hill

N

START HERE

P

Mount Hill

Spring Lane

Cookham Dean Common (N.T.)

Long Lane

Choke Lane

Mount Farm

Butlers Gate

Beeching Grove Wood

Heron's Court

Malders Lane

Cannon Court Farm

Winter Hill Road

Hindhay Farm

To Maidenhead

To Pinkneys Green

0	¼	½ mile
0	¼	½ kilometre

Boundary Stone

Lot Farm
and Ashley Hill Woods

distance 3 miles

This circular walk, of about 3 miles in length, goes out through the fields of Lot Farm and the IGAP (Institute of Grassland and Animal Production) to the summit of Ashley Hill and returns through the fields used for the Knowl Hill Steam Rally.

The directions below start from the lay-by at the 'Seven Stars' on the Bath Road (A4) at Knowl Hill (Grid Ref. 822794), but the map of the route may suggest other starting places. For further topographical features of the area, see the Ordnance Survey 1:25,000 'Pathfinder' series map Sheet 1173 'Windsor' and Sheet 1157 'Maidenhead and Marlow'. Please observe the Country Code.

With your back to the Bath Road, walk along Star Lane to left of 'Seven Stars' and shortly bear right at works entrance. When track soon reaches green, surrounded by several houses, keep straight on to cross stile into field ahead. Now follow short fence on left and maintain same direction up through middle of field to far corner of woodland on right, here bear slightly left to leave field by stile in front of white faced bungalow ahead. Turn left in front of bungalow to pass over stile next to first wooden gate, then immediately turn right along hedged grass track – to your right is the wooded summit of Ashley Hill (474ft.).

Entering field ahead, continue along edge of field with hedge and then woodland on right to pass over stile and sleeper bridge in far corner. Now turn right to follow winding waymarked (painted white arrows) path, through woodland to reach road (Warren Row Road), here turn left along road. Shortly on left is the entrance to a system of chalk tunnels which at one time supplied the finest chalk to the then nearby Whiting Works. More recent uses for the underground site have included a war-time shadow factory and an emergency seat of regional government. Today it is a document store.

When the road turns left, keep straight on, soon along concrete farm track (Hodgedale Lane) between buildings and houses. At end of field on right, follow gravel track through right-hand bend and up gentle climb, then where track turns left to become a concrete road, fork right over stile next to metal gate to continue on gravel track. At top of rise, as track bears left, cross another stile at side of metal gate and continue ahead – here look left for distant views of Warren Row and Pudders Farm. After stile at end of track, continue along edge of field with fence on left, then after further stile and sloping footbridge, turn right along gravel track. Just after cottage on left, fork left into narrow path running parallel to track, then shortly cross this track to enter by stileway, the Forestry Commission's – Ashley Hill Woods.

Continue ahead up steep woodland path, passing over two crossing forest rides, then near top of climb, fork right to pass on left on summit the old 'Keepers Cottage' – sold by auction in 1987 and since then the scene of local controversy over development on the site. Some 45 yards after end of boundary wall, at path junction, keep left winding gently downhill, then where main track turns sharp left, continue ahead on narrowing path to reach stile at edge of woods. Here look left for distant view of Windsor Castle and look ahead for White Waltham and the tall buildings of Bracknell.

Continue down edge of field with hedge on right, then at small copse on right, climb stile ahead and keep along edge of next field with hedge now on left. After stile at end of field, continue down short gulley to another stile, here bear right across tarmac track to enter through metal gate large field opposite – Bottle Meadow, the site used annually since 1971 for the Knowl Hill Steam Rally. The cluster of attractive old buildings on the hill to your right is Lot Farm. Maintain same direction through middle of field to distant stile in hedge, seen just to left of Knowl Hill Church. After stile turn right to reach road, here turn left and then shortly turn right along Bath Road to return to start.

DATE WALKED   19

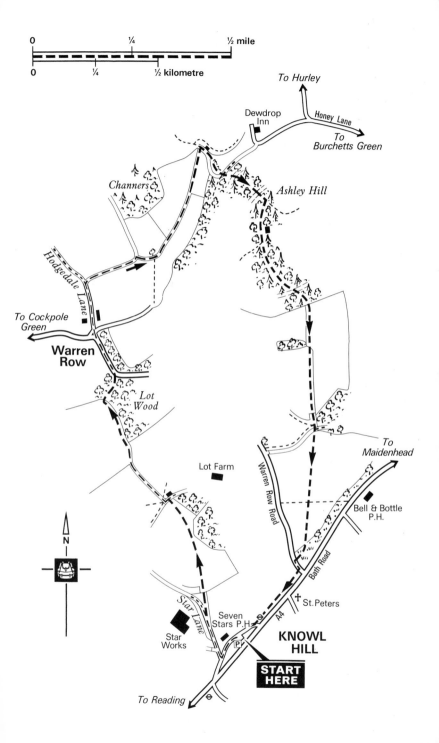

Happy Valley and Bovingdon Green

distance 4 miles

This circular walk, of nearly 4 miles in length, after leaving the built-up area of Marlow, climbs up through Happy Valley into Davenport Woods, passes through the pleasant hamlet of Bovingdon Green and returns along the ridge that gives extensive views over Marlow and the Thames Valley.

The directions below start from the car park in Pound Lane, Marlow (Grid Ref. 848862), but the map of the route may suggest other starting places. For further topographical features of the area, see the Ordnance Survey 1:25,000 'Pathfinder' series map Sheet 1157 'Maidenhead and Marlow'. Please observe the Country Code; in particular, keep to footpaths, keep dogs on lead across farmland and leave all wild flowers for others to enjoy.

With your back to the car park, turn left and starting off along left-hand verge, follow a winding Pound Lane for just over half-a-mile to reach junction with Henley Road (A4155). With great care cross road to enter tarmac track to Beechwood Farm Nursery and after about 80 yards, fork right through metal swing gate into short fenced path, then continue along edge of field with hedge and overhead power lines on left, the start of a gentle climb up through – Happy Valley.

After stile at end of field, keep straight on and at ladder stile at end of fence on left, continue ahead with valley bottom close on left to hidden stile at right-hand end of facing hedge. Keep straight on along wooded path with field below on left to enter Davenport Woods ahead by stile immediately after old pit on right. Continue along woodland track in valley bottom, ignoring track to left after about 300 yards. After a further 60 yards ahead, fork right and after about another 100 yards, turn right into crossing track going uphill past old pit on left. At top of slope, follow concrete post and wire fence, to emerge from woodland over stile into enclosed path, with trees on left. After stile at end of trees, about halfway along second field, enter path with fence on left and hedge on right. On reaching cottages on left, continue along winding gravel track to emerge at the edge of – Bovingdon Green.

Keep straight on along gravel track across the green to junction with Frieth Road ahead, here with care turn right along road keeping up on the wide grass verge on left. About 20 yards along road (now Chalkpit Lane) after 'The Royal Oak', fork left along gravel track and on facing the property 'Blounts Lodge', turn left up tarmac drive for about 20 yards, then turn sharp right into very narrow enclosed path. After passing between concrete posts, follow this fenced path for over quarter-of-a-mile – soon are seen extensive views over Marlow and the Thames Valley.

After next concrete posts, descend more steeply with allotments on left and houses on right. At road on right, bear slightly left down tarmac path and at end of allotments, fork right into another fenced path with garages on right and old people's home below on left. At road, at 'Duke of Cambridge', cross over into Eton Place opposite and at end follow passage between houses. Turn left along road ahead for about 60 yards, then turn right into Riley Recreation Ground and bear slightly left to hidden metal swing gate to left of children's play area. Now turn right along road (not Riley Road into car park) with the terraced 'Sunlight Cottages' on left and at the end of Dukes Place, with great care cross over main road (A4155, Spittal Street) and turn right. Shortly at road junction, turn left down the length of the High Street and on reaching Station Road at the mini round-a-bouts, with care turn right into Pound Lane, past Higginson Park on left, to return to car park at start.

DATE WALKED   19

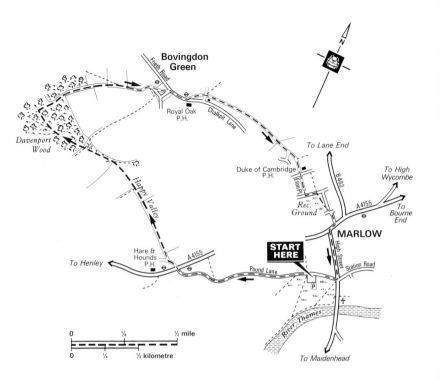

Map labels

Bovingdon Green

Frieth Road

Royal Oak P.H.

Chalkpit Lane

Davenport Wood

Happy Valley

Duke of Cambridge P.H.

To Lane End

To High Wycombe

Eton Pl.

B 482

Rec. Ground

A 4155

To Bourne End

MARLOW

Hare & Hounds P.H.

A 4155

To Henley

START HERE

Pound Lane

High Street

Station Road

P

River Thames

To Maidenhead

| 0 | ¼ | ½ mile |
| 0 | ¼ | ½ kilometre |

Happy Valley.

Pudders Farm and Cayton Park

distance 4 miles

This circular walk, of nearly 4 miles in length, (made possible by a permitted footpath on the Juddmonte Farms) is through the pleasant undulating grazing land around Pudders Farm and the attractive woodland in Cayton Park.

The directions below start from Holly Cross (Grid Ref. 802080), on the west side of the cross-roads (where buses once stopped), but the map of the route may suggest other starting places. For further topographical features of the area, see the Ordnance Survey 1:25,000 'Pathfinder' series map Sheet 1157 'Maidenhead and Marlow'. Please observe the Country Code; in particular, keep to footpaths, keep dogs on lead across farmland and leave all wild flowers for others to enjoy.

With your back to cross-roads and entrance to Cayton Park, follow road using footway on left and at turning to Crazies Hill, keep straight on along verge on right to reach Cockpole Green. At first house on left facing green, 'Hatchgate End' turn half-right across green and then cross road into concrete farm road opposite signposted Public Bridleway. Continue straight on between the buildings of Goulders Farm and then along fenced farm track. The distant large white building among trees in the near Chilterns on the other side of the Thames Valley, is Danesfield, once the home of RAF Medmenham and now an hotel. Ignore field entrance on left to enter gently descending hedged and fenced path to soon have young woodland on left. The buildings in fold of land to your right are Dean Place, the starting point of the earlier Farm Trail, part of that route being used on this walk. At end of trees on left, follow right turn in path for about 30 yards then turn left along Rose Lane.

Just past the South Lodge to Rosehill on left and before top of rise in road, turn right through small wooden swing gate onto descending hedged and fenced tarmac farm road – this is a permitted path, which is the effective answer for the landowner who likes to see genuine ramblers enjoying the countryside – but who nevertheless does not want a right of way established across the land. Follow this track, forking right at junction, then around large right-hand curve with wooded bank on right and fenced paddocks on left to reach small roundabout at top of short climb – here pause and face left. Half-right is the wooded summit (474ft.) of Ashley Hill in the midst of 300 acres of Forestry Commission woodland and slightly left in the near corner of woodland in valley on Hodgedale Lane is the BBONT (Berks Bucks Oxon Naturalists Trust) Hurley Chalk Pit. Continue along tarmac road through left-hand bend to reach right-hand bend, here turn sharp left over stile, but pause for distant view ahead of the beautifully restored buildings of – Pudders Farm.

Follow descending path with hedge and fence on right to reach Hodgedale Lane after three stiles close together, here you turn right and have a choice of route. Either keep to sunken hedged bridleway or preferably retrace your steps over last stile and enter the higher grass path between fences. At end of third field, at stile on left, turn half right through middle of young copse to soon reach, and then follow, the wooden fence of paddock on right. At far end of field continue in same direction to cross stile into short enclosed path. Cross stile next to wooden gate and continue on gravel drive to reach road at Warren Row. With care turn right along road for about 60 yards, then turn left into track between houses and after garages on right, enter woodland path ahead leading into – Cayton Park.

Continue straight on, climbing well-defined and waymarked (painted white arrows) woodland path, bearing slightly right just after break in trees. At top of climb, the summit (460ft.) of Bowsey Hill, pass through large wooden gate and turn right down single track road to return to Holly Cross and the start.

DATE WALKED _____ 19 _____

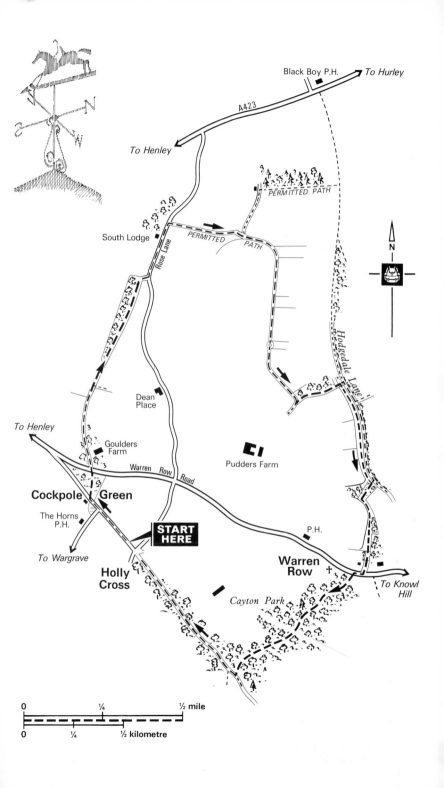

Three Greens Walk

distance 4^1/$_2$ miles

This circular walk, of about 4^1/$_2$ miles in length, includes the south-west perimeter of Maidenhead Thicket and the rich agricultural land beyond. The walk also provides the opportunity to see four of the 1934 Maidenhead Borough boundary stones.

The directions below start from the National Trust parking place in Cannon Lane, which is situated immediately south of, and adjacent to, the motorway spur A423(M) (Grid Ref. 859803), but the map of the route may suggest other starting places or shorter alternatives. For further topographical features of the area, see the Ordnance Survey 1:25,000 'Pathfinder' series maps Sheet1157 'Maidenhead and Marlow' and 1173 'Windsor'. Please observe the Country Code.

With your back to the roads, take broad grass ride ahead along edge of Maidenhead Thicket with hedge and row of trees on left. Where ride devides, keep straight on past houses on left to shortly reach 'Thicket Lodge'. Cross over tarmac road and bear slightly right along woodland path, then after steeply descending steps (originally cut in 1975 by scouts of the Maidenhead Boyne Hill troop) pass along left-hand edge of old pit to wooden swing gate at road (Cherry Garden Lane). Now turn left past Woolley Firs Conservation Trust on left and continue along road for about a quarter of a mile, then just after passing under overhead power lines, opposite large cream painted house - 'Altmore ', turn right up bank to enter field by stile. Go straight ahead on grass path through middle of fields to soon reach and follow power lines and hedge on right. Cross new road with stiles both sides and where field boundary bears slightly left – look right for summit (474ft.) of Ashley Hill and left for distant spire of Shottesbrooke Church – then continue ahead. On reaching facing hedge, turn right along hedged farm track and the road to arrive at south end of – Littlewick Green.

Passing the white painted property 'Red Roofs' on right (once the home of Ivor Novello), follow right-hand edge of green and on approaching small group of trees, bear left across green to then follow road to reach junction with main road (A4). With great care cross over and go straight ahead along gravel track, Green Lane, then after nursery on right, continue on narrow gravel path. On reaching road (Burchetts Green Lane), opposite large white house, turn left – keeping to right-hand side to face oncoming traffic. Just after large house, 'Stubbings Manor', on right, where road bends left to Burchetts Green, turn right through metal swing gate into Stubbings Farm.

Passing between hedge on left and barn on right, keep straight ahead on track along edge of large field with hedge on right at first. At end of field on left, enter short fenced path over stile and after two more stiles close together, continue ahead through narrow field with row of large chestnut trees on left. After two stiles at far end of field next to 'Stubbings Lodge', turn right into broad woodland path along edge of Maidenhead Thicket. Within yards fork right, keeping fence close on right to soon see on right, 'Stubbings House' – the residence used by Queen Wilhelmina of the Netherlands during the Second World War. Continue along edge of woodland, then just before end of field on right look for first boundary stone adjacent to wire fence on right, the other three stones (see map) are on south side of A4 (Bath Road) where you cross, at foot of hedge to garden of 'Shire Horse' and 10 feet to left of entrance to 'Heathside Cottage'. Continue on for a further 20 yards, then turn half left into a narrower woodland path, and after second horse barrier, keep right to reach A4 again, opposite the 'Shire Horse' at – Woolley Green.

With great care cross over A4 and bear slightly left along tarmac road, then shortly, about 20 yards after crossroads, turn left into woodland and follow this well-defined path to eventually return to parking place at start.

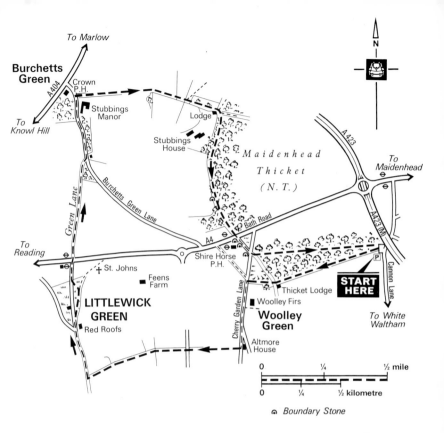

To Marlow

Burchetts Green

To Knowl Hill

Crown P.H.

Stubbings Manor

Lodge

Stubbings House

Maidenhead Thicket (N.T.)

To Maidenhead

Bath Road

Burchetts Green Lane

Green Lane

To Reading

A4

Shire Horse P.H.

+ St. Johns

Feens Farm

LITTLEWICK GREEN

Red Roofs

Cherry Garden Lane

Thicket Lodge

Woolley Firs

Woolley Green

START HERE

Cannon Lane

To White Waltham

Altmore House

N

| 0 | ¼ | ½ mile |
| 0 | ¼ | ½ kilometre |

⊙ *Boundary Stone*

Young Shire Horses outside 'their' Pub !

Star Lane and Bowsey Hill

distance 3 miles

This circular walk, of about 3 miles in length, includes the attractive woodland path through Cayton Park and the paths through the Knowl Hill sand pits. The route is over well used paths, but in winter and after wet weather go well shod, as you could find a few short but extremely muddy patches. Should progress prove particularly difficult under foot in the early part of the walk at the end of the firm surface of Star Lane, see map for alternative route to the east.

The directions below start from the lay-by at the 'Seven Stars' on the Bath Road (A4) at Knowl Hill (Grid Ref. 822794),but the map of the route may suggest other starting places. For further topographical features of the area, see the Ordnance Survey 1:25,000 'Pathfinder' series maps Sheet 1173 'Windsor' and Sheet 1157 'Maidenhead and Marlow'. Please observe the Country Code; in particular, keep to footpaths, keep dogs on lead across farmland and leave all wild flowers for others to enjoy.

With your back to the Bath Road, walk along Star Lane to left of 'Seven Stars' and shortly bear right at works entrance. When track soon reaches green, turn left at first pair of modern houses on right, to continue on unsurfaced track climbing slowly - Star Lane.

After last house 'Meadow View' on right, continue ahead on woodland track. Ignore paths turning left and right and go straight on, to cross low wooden rail. Here look right for the summit (474ft.) of Ashley Hill in the midst of 300 acres of Forestry Commission woodland and over your right shoulder for distant view of Windsor Castle. On eventually reaching further wooden rail, keep straight on along gravel track to road (Warren Row Road) ahead opposite 'The Warrener Restaurant' (which until 1981 was the 'Red House' public house), here with care turn left along road into Warren Row. After about 100 yards, turn left into tarmac track between houses and after garages on right enter woodland path ahead leading into Cayton Park. Continue

straight on climbing well-defined and waymarked (painted white arrows) woodland path, bearing slightly right just after break in trees. At top of climb, pass through large wooden gate to reach tarmac track at the summit (460ft.) of – Bowsey Hill.

Now turn left to where tarmac ends, then keep straight ahead along broad woodland track and at both signposted path junctions, keep left all the time with woodland fence and bank on left. After descending slowly on woodland path for about mile, look out for metal and concrete stile, here fork right to descend more steeply to reach a further metal/concrete stile. Emerging from woodland, continue along broad grass strip, then hedged path between quarry workings. Between pits keep sharp lookout for hoof prints of deer in any soft ground.

At end of pits cross over broad track and enter narrow woodland path (Canhurst Lane) ahead for about 50 yards – here is a choice of route for the remainder of the walk. For the first choice, go straight on along broad grass tree-lined ride and after passing through metal swing gate continue down gravel drive. At main road (A4) ahead, opposite 'The Old Devil Inn', turn left along road to return to the start.

For the second choice, turn left passing rear entrance of works on right to descend a steep, fenced and tree-lined path. After crossing floor of sand pit, climb up to metal and concrete stile to reach Star Lane once more, here turn right to return to the start.

DATE WALKED | | 19

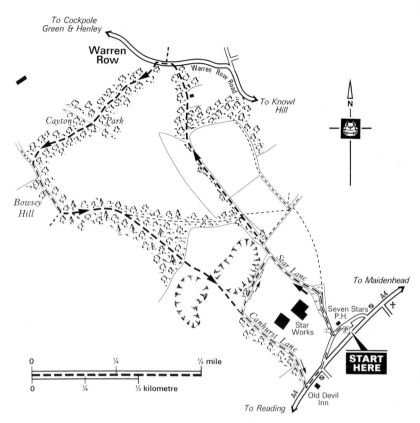

To Cockpole
Green & Henley

Warren
Row

Warren Row Road

To Knowl
Hill

N

Cayton Park

Bowsey
Hill

Star Lane

To Maidenhead

A4

Star Works

Seven Stars
P.H.

P

START HERE

Canhurst Lane

To Reading

A4

Old Devil
Inn

0   ¼   ½ mile

0   ¼   ½ kilometre

The Dew Drop Inn (Ramble No. 16)

Hardings Green and Winter Hill

distance 3 ¹/₂ miles

This circular walk, of about 3¹/₂ miles in length, after leaving the built-up area of Cookham Rise, climbs up through the farmland around Cookham Dean and returns along part of the Winter Hill ridge and across the John Lewis Golf Course. Also described is a slightly longer route of about 4 miles.

The directions below start from Cookham Station approach (Grid Ref. 887850) where there is room to park, but the map of the route may suggest other starting places. For further topographical features of the area, see the Ordnance Survey 1:25,000 'Pathfinder' series map Sheet 1157 'Maidenhead and Marlow'. Please observe the Country Code.

From entrance to Cookham Station, turn left over level crossing then immediately turn left again at 'The Railway Tavern' to follow the length of High Road, passing on left just after Primary School at corner of Worster Road, 'Cliveden View', the house where the well-known local artist Sir Stanley Spencer CBE RA worked and lived from l944-58. Cross over Whyteladyes Lane ahead and here is the choice of route.

For the longer walk, with the opportunity to visit the attractive l9th century flint-faced St. John the Baptists' Church at Cookham Dean, keep ahead on gravel farm track (Kennel Lane) to the church, there turn right and follow winding road past war memorial and through Hardings Green to rejoin shorter walk at 'Uncle Tom's Cabin'. For the shorter walk, turn right along road for about 100 yards, then turn left through opening to follow narrow path with wire fences both sides. After Cricket Ground turn left to pass through swing gate and climb wide stony path up middle of field to reach concrete stile to right of gateway. At this point, pause for distant views of the Thames Valley, Cliveden Reach woods and on a clear day, Ascot Grandstand, before continuing on gravel track to emerge at – Hardings Green (NT). Now go right to 'Uncle Tom's Cabin' then immediately fork left down the narrow Warners Hill. At

'Fairhill' fork left to descend through woodland strip. At foot of hill, with care turn left, then in about 25 yards turn right alongside garden boundary of property. 'Warners', (not the parallel track), to enter enclosed path in gully. Continue ahead across grass strip to reach stile at top of climb. Keep straight on through middle of field to further stile. Here go straight ahead, between wooden posts and pass to right of small barn. At end of track, with care turn right along road – but turn left if you wish to make a detour to visit the top of – Winter Hill (NT).

Shortly, opposite property 'Chimneys', fork left down gravel track to pass over concrete stile to left of metal gate to enter Cockmarsh (NT) – l32 acres of flat marshy meadows and steep chalk slopes. After about 150 yards, fork right off track keeping close for a while to fence on right, then emerging on to open hill top (with fine views over the Spade Oak and Bourne End reaches of the river) continue along ridge with trees nearby on right. When field fence appears clearly at top of ridge on right, soon look out for stile in fence, then turn right steeply up slope and after stile, follow edge of field with hedge and golf course on left.

After stile near end of field, immediately turn left over another stile and along edge of golf course with hedge on right. At end of hedge, pause for a glimpse of Cookham with its bridge and Cliveden House (NT) among trees on distant ridge, before continuing straight on passing to left of brown corrugated building to reach distant bridge over railway line ahead. When over bridge turn right, but bear slightly left away from railway to left-hand end of hedge ahead, here bear right keeping to edge of golf course with wire fence on right to reach stile, then continue on broad track to reach Terry's Lane. With care turn left along road for about 20 yards, then turn right into gravel track, Poundfield Lane, to eventually reach 'The Gate' at junction of The Pound and Maidenhead Road, here turn right along Station Hill to return to the start.

A frosty morning on Winter Hill.

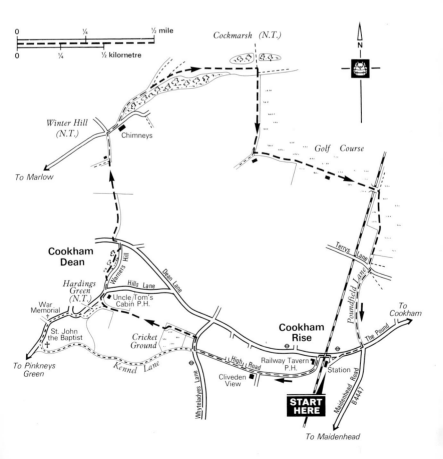

Cockmarsh (N.T.)

N

0   ¼   ½ mile

0   ¼   ½ kilometre

Winter Hill
(N.T.)

Chimneys

To Marlow

Golf Course

Cookham Dean

Warners Hill

Hills Lane

Dean Lane

Terrys Lane

Hardings Green (N.T.)

War Memorial

Uncle Tom's Cabin P.H.

St. John the Baptist

Cricket Ground

To Pinkneys Green

Kennel Lane

Whyteladyes Lane

High Road

Cliveden View

Cookham Rise

Railway Tavern P.H.

Station

Poundfield Lane

The Pound

To Cookham

Maidenhead Road

B4447

START HERE

To Maidenhead

Top Farm and Hodgedale Lane

distance 3$^1/_2$ miles

This circular walk, of about 3$^1/_2$ miles in length, (made possible by a permitted footpath at Hall Place), goes out through the fields farmed by the Berkshire College of Agriculture and the Institute of Grassland and Animal Production, and returns via the summit of Ashley Hill.

The directions below start from the bend in Honey Lane, near Burchetts Green (Grid Ref. 830813), by an entrance to Ashley Hill Woods (part of the Forestry Commission's Bramshill Forest), but the map of the route may suggest other starting places. For several years there was a parking area at the start, an amenity the Ramblers' Association would like to see restored.

For further topographical features of the area, see the Ordnance Survey 1:25,000 'Pathfinder' series map Sheet 1157 'Maidenhead and Marlow'. Please observe the Country Code.

With your back to lane, walk up tarmac track for 50 yards to enter Ashley Hill Woods by stileway to side of gate. Within a further 15 yards bear right along broad ride through woodland. At a point level with white painted cottage, on other side of lane to right, fork right down narrow path to roadside, opposite Ladyplace Cottages . With care cross road to enter field by small concrete bridge and stile, then follow edge of field with fence and hedge on right to another stile by large tree at bottom of field. Here look over your right shoulder into adjacent field to see brick pyramid built over a well and group of trees, once part of a scene created by Sir George Clayton East, depicting the arrangements of the fleet at the Battle of the Nile.

Continue ahead, but before passing over wooden bridge and stile, look left for a 'swallow-hole' where the stream disappears underground. Keep straight on through middle of next field to stile at concrete farm road, here turn left along road – this is a permitted path , which is the effective answer for the landowner who likes to see genuine ramblers enjoying the countryside – but who nevertheless does not want a right of way established across the land. At road junction ahead, turn left along road (Honey Lane) to pass on right the buildings of – Top Farm.

At end of brick wall on right, turn right past cottages to follow concrete bearing right across farmyard. At end of low building on right, turn right for some 15 yards before turning left, to follow broad hedged track. On reaching junction with concrete farm road, turn left along it to end of woodland on left. Here, where road turns sharp left, keep straight on down edge of fields with fence on left. After stile at bottom, turn left along sunken bridleway – Hodgedale Lane – an ancient cart-way once used by milkmen, bakers, grocers etc., to drive their traps from the main Henley Road to Warren Row village.

Follow bridleway (see map for parallel footpath) for nearly half-a-mile to reach gravel farm track, here turn left on track climbing slowly, then when track turns left to become a concrete road, fork right over stile next to metal gate to continue on gravel track. At top of rise, a few yards in front of next metal gate, turn right over stile and down through middle of field to another stile, in hedge. Bear slightly right at this point, cross two small fields to reach stile next to wooden gate to left of house (The Warren). About 15 yards after stile, turn left up woodland path to shortly reach stile and continue straight on to stileway at boundary of Ashley Hill Woods, here bear slightly right to climb up through woodland. At path junction at top of hill (the 474ft. summit) turn left to pass on right the site of a delightful Victorian 'Keepers Cottage'. The cottage stood empty from 1973 until finally demolished in 1991, following a long planning battle, after controversial development had devastated this once beautiful spot. Shortly at path junction, turn sharp right back towards top of hill to reach tarmac track, here turn left along track downhill to return to the start.

Ramble No.8

DATE WALKED | | 19

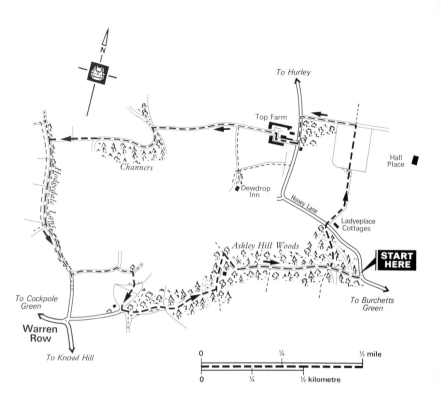

To Hurley

Top Farm

Hall Place

Channers

Hodgedale Lane

Dewdrop Inn

Honey Lane

Ladyeplace Cottages

Ashley Hill Woods

START HERE

To Cockpole Green

Warren Row

To Knowl Hill

To Burchetts Green

| 0 | ¼ | ½ mile |
| 0 | ¼ | ½ kilometre |

Near Warren Row.

Highfield Farm and Crazies Hill

distance 4 miles

This circular walk, of about 4 miles in length, is through pleasant undulating farmland to the north of Wargrave.

The directions below start from the junction of Purfield Drive and Blakes Road, Upper Wargrave (Grid Ref. 792791), but the map of the route may suggest shorter alternatives or other starting places, e.g. from lower end of Highfield Road where there is a wide verge just west of where route crosses road. For visitors to Wargrave parking is suggested on the verge at south end of Crazies Hill Road. For further topographical features of the area, see the Ordnance Survey 1:25,000 'Pathfinder' series maps Sheet 1172 'Reading' and 1156 'Henley-on-Thames'. Please observe the Country Code.

With your back to Purfield Drive, turn right along Blakes Road and in about 50 yards turn left through metal swing gate to follow well-defined path through middle of field to another swing gate at left-hand end of copse ahead. Now follow edge of next field with copse on right to sleeper bridge and further metal swing gate, here keep straight on in following field with fence and ditch on right. About three-quarters of way along this field, pass over stile next to gateway on right, then continue along edge of adjacent field with hedge and soon woods on left. After stile in corner of field, pass over end of hedged green lane and after about 75 yards into next field, turn left over stile into woods (Bottom Boles Wood). Shortly cross sleeper footbridge and follow climbing path, via wooden walk-way, up through woodland with fields nearby on left. After stile at top of climb (at path junction) go diagonally through middle of field to stile next to metal gate at road, here turn right along road passing on right – Highfield Farm.

Shortly, at entrance to property 'Maplecroft' on left, climb bank on left to pass through metal gate and to follow narrow path parallel with road below. At end of enclosed path, cross stile and bear slightly left down through centre of field to a metal gate, in middle of far field boundary. Keep straight on through small woodland, crossing three little springs and a stile to enter short path leading to junction with broader path, Rebecca's Lane. To continue walk turn left, but first turn right for about 25 yards to visit on left, Rebecca's Well – a spring which used to be the hamlet's water supply. In 1870, the Curate of Wargrave, the Rev. Greville Phillimore, invited subscriptions to fund the present structure over the bowl to keep out fallen leaves, etc. At road ahead, with care turn right up road into – Crazies Hill.

At top of climb, opposite the Village Hall, turn sharp left into very narrow fenced path . The large white property, 'Summerfield House', shortly to be seen on right, was formerly Henley Town Hall, dismantled and reconstructed on this site at end of last century to make way for a new building in the town to commemorate Queen Victoria's Jubilee.

Rebecca's Well.

Ramble No.9

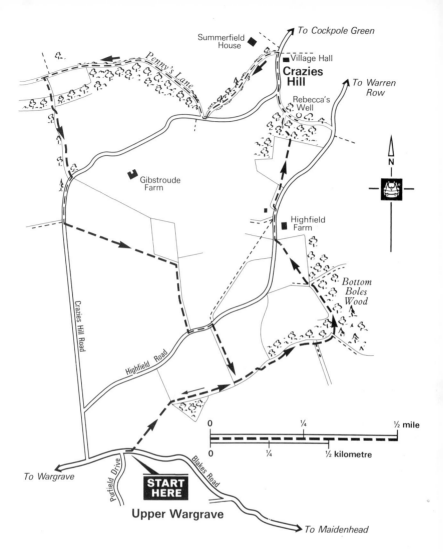

after further stile at top, maintain same direction in next field with fence and trees on right to reach stile at road. Now turn right along road for about 200 yards, Follow path along wooden walk-way and continue through middle of long narrow woodland strip to another stile at road, here turn sharp right down broad sunken stony track – Penny's Lane.

Follow track for about half-a-mile to where stiles appear almost opposite, on either side of the lane, here turn left over stile and steeply up edge of field with fence on left to another stile. Keep straight on up edge of small wood and

then turn left over stile next to metal gate to follow well-defined path through middle of large field. In far corner, turn right to continue along edge of field with fence on left to reach stile next to metal gate at road, then turn left along road (Highfield Road) for about 100 yards before turning right through metal swing gate. Keep along edge of field with fence on right to meet metal swing gate and sleeper bridge used on outward journey, here turn right and retrace your steps to return to start.

DATE WALKED | | 19

Castle End and Mumberry Hill

distance 4 miles

This circular walk, of about 4 miles in length, is through the rich agricultural land that lies between Twyford and Wargrave. The small parish of Ruscombe is visited, with its attractive church of St. James the Great – erected in flint and stone at the end of the 12th century, its nave and tower were rebuilt in brick in 1639 with the weathervane bearing the date.

The directions below start from the south side of Ruscombe Church (Grid Ref. 798763), but the map of the route may suggest other starting places. For further topographical features of the area, see the Ordnance Survey 1:25,000 'Pathfinder' series maps Sheet 1172 'Reading' and 1173 'Windsor'. Please observe the Country Code; in particular, keep to footpaths, keep dogs on lead across farmland and leave all wild flowers for others to enjoy.

Facing east, with the church of St. James the Great on your left, bear right into 'no through road', Southbury Lane, to cross over railway – the main Western Region line. At bottom of hill, immediately after red-brick farmhouse on left, turn left over stile and along edge of small field to end of hedge on left, here turn left in next field to follow ditch and trees on left. On facing railway embankment in corner of field, turn right and then immediately fork left up bank, to continue with railway fence close on left. Just past railway signal, bear slightly right to descend steps (built in 1979 by local members of the Ramblers' Association) to road (B3024) after stile. With care turn left along road to pass under railway, Girder Bridge, then immediately turn right through gap next to metal field gate and along gravel farm track with fence on right towards – Castle End.

On approaching Castle End Farm fork left to shortly face red brick houses, here turn left along road (Castle End Road). After about 150 yards, turn right over stile next to metal field gate, then bear right through middle of field, passing just to right of first electricity pole, to white

waymarks at middle of woodland ahead. Keep straight on through woodland with fence soon on left, then after stile at end of woodland, continue along fenced path to another stile, here bear slightly right along fenced track to reach road. Now turn left along road, Milley Lane, to 'The Horse and Groom', here with great care cross over main road (A4) and turn left to shortly pass along the length of Kennedy's Nurseries on the right – if open, why not wander through and have a look! At road junction, fork right along the B477 – Mumberry Hill.

Continue along road for about half-a-mile keeping to narrow footway on left to reach, after third house - 'Stonecrest' - set back on right, bridleway track on left. If you would like to rest awhile at this point, go ahead for about 200 yards to find bench seat on left. To continue walk, turn left into this bridleway track, straight through middle of field – here look right for distant views of Reading. At main road (A4) ahead (the once well-known Waterers Floral Mile) with great care cross over into fenced track opposite, then keep straight on along edge of field with conifers on left.

Ruscombe Church.

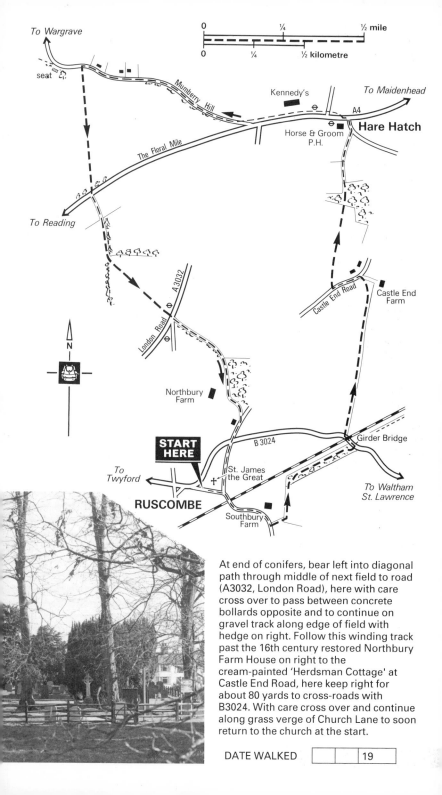

To Wargrave

seat

0 ¼ ½ mile
0 ¼ ½ kilometre

Mumbery Hill

Kennedy's

To Maidenhead

A4

Hare Hatch

Horse & Groom P.H.

The Floral Mile

To Reading

A3032

London Road

Castle End Road

Castle End Farm

Northbury Farm

START HERE

B 3024

Girder Bridge

To Twyford

St. James the Great

To Waltham St. Lawrence

RUSCOMBE

Southbury Farm

N

At end of conifers, bear left into diagonal path through middle of next field to road (A3032, London Road), here with care cross over to pass between concrete bollards opposite and to continue on gravel track along edge of field with hedge on right. Follow this winding track past the 16th century restored Northbury Farm House on right to the cream-painted 'Herdsman Cottage' at Castle End Road, here keep right for about 80 yards to cross-roads with B3024. With care cross over and continue along grass verge of Church Lane to soon return to the church at the start.

DATE WALKED   19

Downfield Lane and Shottesbrooke Park

distance 3¹/₂ miles

This circular walk, of about 3¹/₂ miles in length, goes out through the farmland south of Waltham St. Lawrence village and returns through part of the beautiful Shottesbrooke Park. In winter, a few places can be rather muddy, so do go suitably shod. The waymarking (painted white arrows) to be seen, is the work of members of the Ramblers' Association.

The directions below start from Waltham St. Lawrence Parish Church (Grid Ref. 829769), but the map of the route may suggest other starting places. Seen near the church are the 14th century 'Bell Inn' and the 'Neville Hall', both given to the village by the Newberry family who once lived in a moated manor house at Beenhams. For further topographical features of the area, see the Ordnance Survey 1:25,000 'Pathfinder' series map Sheet 1173 'Windsor'. Please observe the Country Code; in particular, keep to footpaths, keep dogs on lead across farmland and leave all wild flowers for others to enjoy.

With your back to the picturesque flint-faced part-11th century church of St. Lawrence, from The Pound turn right along road, then immediately bear left into Neville Close. At trees ahead, turn left through middle of field to a point on far boundary just to right of shed. Staying in same field, turn right and then left along edge of field with hedge on left to reach small wooden bridge with stile. Bear slightly right through middle of next field to reach double stile and sleeper bridge at road to right of houses ahead.

With care turn left along road for about 10 yards, then turn right over stile and through middle of field along a line of the remains of an old hedge to stile and sleeper bridge at road. Turn right along road using footway on left, then just before the narrow Sill Bridge turn left over stile into small field to soon reach another stile just ahead. Continue straight on through middle of three fields to stile at far boundary, here enter path between rear of houses on left and deep water channel on right to reach road at

Crockford's Bridge by Shurlock Row sign. Cross over road and turn right into road just ahead, then after about 30 yards turn left into hedged track – Downfield Lane.

Follow this track for nearly three quarters of a mile, to where the track bends left, here keep straight on over stile diagonally through middle of narrow field. Leave field through gateway along grass track and shortly continue past white cottage on left on gravel track – shown on old maps as the north end of Pundles Lane. With care at road (B3024, Broadmoor Lane) ahead, cross over and turn right for about 15 yards, then turn left into – Shottesbrooke Park.

Keep fence on left to reach the 14th century church of St. John the Baptist – thought to be a scaled down version of Salisbury Cathedral – turn left through metal swing gate into churchyard. Legend says that when the church was completed in 1337, pleased with his work, the architect climbed to the top of the spire to toast his work with a glass of wine – unfortunately he lost his balance, fell to his death and was buried on the spot. Continuing through churchyard into walled path, look through gap in wall on right for glimpse of lawns up to the 16th century Shottesbrooke House – the home of Sir John Smith C.B.E., the first Freeman of the new Royal Borough of Windsor and Maidenhead and founder in 1965 of the Landmark Trust.

When through brick arch, go ahead over stile to follow edge of field with 'ha-ha' (fence in bottom of ditch) on right. After stile next to wooden gate, follow path along field edge and then through trees ahead (Burringham Wood), to eventually reach stile at road (Halls Lane). Now turn right along road, then immediately after passing Halls Farm on right, turn left into short gravel track. At entrance to cemetery, turn right into hedged and fenced path to reach road ahead, here turn left along road to return to the start.

DATE WALKED · 19

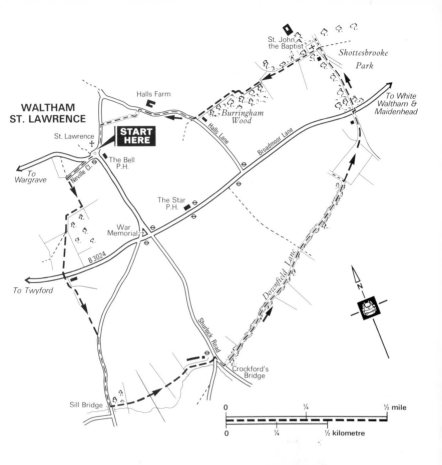

WALTHAM
ST. LAWRENCE

Halls Farm

START HERE

St. Lawrence

To Wargrave

The Bell P.H.

Neville Cl.

The Star P.H.

War Memorial

B 3024

To Twyford

Shurlock Road

Sill Bridge

Crockford's Bridge

Dorinfield Lane

Halls Lane

Broadmoor Lane

Burringham Wood

St. John the Baptist

Shottesbrooke Park

To White Waltham & Maidenhead

N

| 0 | ¼ | ½ mile |
| 0 | ¼ | ½ kilometre |

The footpath and Ha-Ha alongside the garden of Shottesbrook House.

Stroud Farm and Gays Lane

distance 3^1/$_2$ miles

This flat circular walk, of about 3^1/$_2$ miles in length, after leaving the built-up area, is through the pleasant pastures and arable land between Holyport and Fifield – the entire walk being within the Parish of Bray. By taking a short cut along Coningsby Lane, it is possible to reduce the length of the walk to about 2 miles.

The directions below start from the War Memorial on Holyport Green (Grid Ref. 892778), but the map of the route may suggest other starting places. For further topographical features of the area, see the Ordnance Survey 1:25,000 'Pathfinder' series map Sheet 1173 'Windsor'. Please observe the Country Code; in particular, keep to footpaths, keep dogs on lead across farmland and leave all wild flowers for others to enjoy.

Facing the War Memorial, enter 'no through road', Holyport Street, passing pond and the wisteria-clad 'Belgian Arms' on right to stile at end of road. In field, turn right to another stile at road (Holyport Road). With care, cross over road and continue straight on along the length of Stroud Farm Road and the private road up to – Stroud Farm.

On reaching farm buildings turn left along farm track passing long low cart-shed on left. At entrance to field ahead, immediately after crossing drainage ditch, turn right over stile into fenced path with ditch on right and restored gravel workings on left. After stile and concrete footbridge ahead, keep right with pond on right along fenced grass path around edge of field passing through one right-hand and two left-hand bends. After passing over stile and wooden footbridge ahead, turn right along edge of field with hedge on right. Cross stile in wire fence and leave field by stile next to metal gate, entering short hedged path leading to Coningsby Lane. Here turn left along road to continue walk or turn right for the shorter walk.

At road junction ahead, with care turn right along road (keeping to right-hand side) past the 'Hare & Hounds' on left, then about 50 yards after Stewart Close on right, turn right into tarmac track to property 'Deep Meadows' . Very shortly, at second set of white brick pillars, turn left into path between trees on left and fence on right – the whole length of this path was completely overgrown and impenetrable in 1971, when it was cleared by members of the then newly formed East Berks Group of the Ramblers' Association. Look out for unusual sight along here - an 0-4-0 saddle tank engine! Emerging at end of gravel track, Ledger Lane, go ahead for about 15 yards, then turn right through small copse to stile next to field gate, here continue straight on to soon follow edge of field with fence on left. After sleeper footbridge with two stiles, bear slightly right through middle of next field to stile in hedge in middle of far boundary at road - Coningsby Lane. Now turn right along and just after first buildings (Coningsby Farm) on left (rejoining shorter route here) turn left into broad gravel hedged track – Green Lane.

After 125 yards, pass over stile on right, then turn half-left to soon follow edge of field with hedge on left and to reach sleeper footbridge with two stiles. Continue along edge of next field with hedge on left, then after further sleeper footbridge and stile, keep straight on to follow near edge of field with several oak trees on right. At far end of field, after stile and sleeper footbridge, turn right along broad gravel track – Gays Lane. The whole length of this path between Green Lane and Gays Lane was completely obstructed in 1975 until local members of the Ramblers' Association constructed all the stiles and footbridges.

At end of track turn left along road (Langworthy Lane) for about 150 yards, then turn right over small concrete footbridge and along edge of the garden to 'Foxes Glee' into fenced and hedged path – known locally as the 'Click-Clack'. Emerging at road, continue ahead across Holyport Green to return to the start.

Ramble No. 12

DATE WALKED | | 19

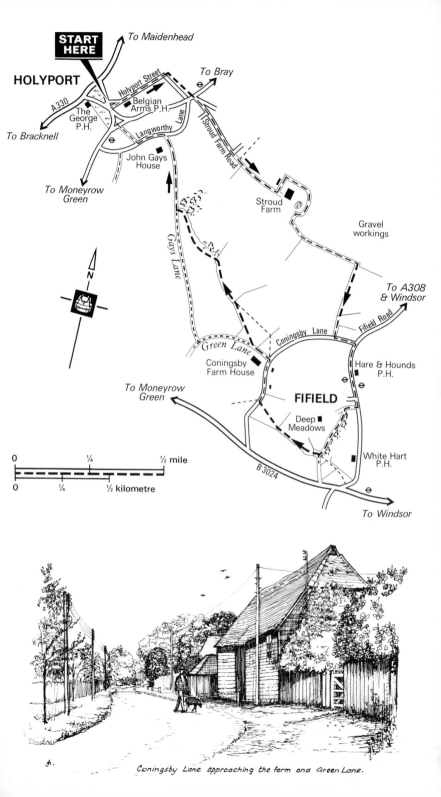

START HERE

To Maidenhead

HOLYPORT

To Bray

A330

Holyport Street

Belgian Arms P.H.

The George P.H.

To Bracknell

Langworthy

Lane

Stroud Farm Road

John Gays House

To Moneyrow Green

Gays Lane

Stroud Farm

Gravel workings

N

To A308 & Windsor

Coningsby Lane

Fifield Road

Green Lane

Coningsby Farm House

Hare & Hounds P.H.

To Moneyrow Green

FIFIELD

Deep Meadows

White Hart P.H.

B 3024

To Windsor

| 0 | | ¼ | | ½ mile |
| 0 | | ¼ | | ½ kilometre |

Coningsby Lane approaching the farm and Green Lane.

Stud Green and Blackbird Lane

distance 4 miles

This flat circular walk, of about 4 miles in length, is through the rich agricultural land between Holyport Green and Touchen End. If doing this walk during the winter, the early part of the route can be rather wet, so do go suitably shod.

The directions below start from the War Memorial on Holyport Green (Grid Ref. 892778), but the map of the route may suggest other starting places or shorter alternatives. For further topographical features of the area, see the Ordnance Survey 1:25,000 'Pathfinder' series map Sheet1173 'Windsor'. Please observe the Country Code; in particular, keep to footpaths, keep dogs on lead across farmland and leave all wild flowers for others to enjoy.

With your back to the War Memorial, turn half right across the middle of Holyport Green and cross road to enter path by stile to left of white painted house (formerly 'The Cricketers'). Shortly, after concrete footbridge and another stile, keep along edge of field with hedge on right, then after further stile continue along edge of next field with hedge now on left. At end of field, after sleeper footbridge with two stiles, continue along edge of field with fence on left to pass over a further sleeper footbridge with two stiles. Follow field edge through left and right-hand bends, then in next corner of field turn left over stile and bear right along edge of field with hedge and fence on right. After further stile ahead, continue along gravel track (Meadow View Lane) to reach road at – Stud Green.

Now turn right along road for about 100 yards, then turn left into gravel road (Rolls Lane) and at end of this, at 'Lemor Cottage', bear left to follow ditch and hedge close on left. Cross stile into large field to follow wire fence and ditch on left. Shortly before end of field, turn left into gateway, cross stile and go half right through middle of two fields to stile at road (A330) in far corner. At road, cross over and turn right along tarmac footway, then immediately after 'The Poplars' cottages on left, turn left into

concrete farm road and where this swings left, turn left into grass path with fence on left and row of conifers on right. Shortly follow this path through right-hand bend and eventually at end of conifers, turn right along farm track – Long Lane.

Immediately after isolated white painted cottage on left, turn left through grassed area to follow garden fence on left. Maintain same direction through middle of field, following hedge now on right. In corner of field, turn right into next field with fence on left, then shortly follow field boundary through left-hand bend with deep ditch now on left. At end of field turn right for few yards before passing over footbridge. Cross end of small field and after further small footbridge, turn left over white painted concrete bridge and along track - Blackbird Lane.

On reaching road (B3024), with care turn right along road for about 120 yards using verge on right and immediately after Old Beams Kennels, turn left into hedged track – Primrose Lane. This once sunken lane, up until 1977 was badly overgrown and in places waterlogged for most of the year, but after local members of the Ramblers' Association had cleared all the overgrowth, the County Council were persuaded to fill in the lane to restore the path to use again. Follow this lane for well over mile and soon after pond on right, turn left over footbridge into broad fenced path along edge of field. At road ahead cross over into Bartletts Lane opposite which continues as a tree lined track and on reaching main road (A330) ahead, turn right along gravel footpath along edge of Holyport Green to return to the start.

DATE WALKED | | 19 |

Ramble No.13

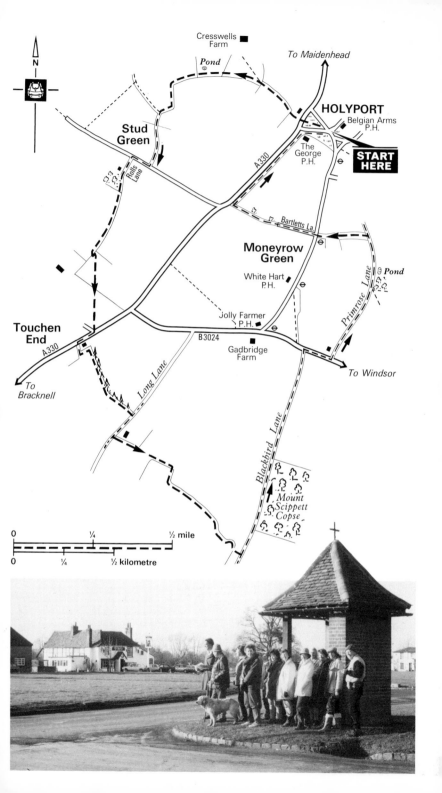

N

Cresswells Farm

Pond

To Maidenhead

HOLYPORT

Belgian Arms P.H.

Stud Green

The George P.H.

START HERE

Rolls Lane

A330

Bartletts La.

Moneyrow Green

Primrose Lane

Pond

White Hart P.H.

Jolly Farmer P.H.

Touchen End

A330

B3024

Gadbridge Farm

To Windsor

To Bracknell

Long Lane

Blackbird Lane

Mount Scippett Copse

0		¼		½ mile

0	¼		½ kilometre	

Love Walk and Snowball Hill

distance 3$\frac{1}{2}$ miles

This circular route, of about 3$\frac{1}{2}$ miles in length, on the very outskirts of Maidenhead, is through the fields and rich farmland between Woodlands Park and White Waltham. The route at Paley Street Farm follows the line of an agreed proposed diversion which avoids walking alongside the M4 motorway.

The directions below start from the small car park (by kind permission of Sir John Smith C.B.E., of Shottesbrooke Park) in White Waltham, opposite the property 'The Red House' (Grid Ref. 850774), but the map of the route may suggest other starting places (e.g. Woodlands Park Avenue). For further topographical features of the area, see the Ordnance Survey 1:25,000 'Pathfinder' series map Sheet 1173 'Windsor'. Please observe the Country Code; in particular, keep to footpaths, keep dogs on lead across farmland and leave all wild flowers for others to enjoy.

With you back to car park, turn left along road (Waltham Road), then about 50 yards after passing road on left (Cherry Garden Lane) turn right across road to enter field by wooden swing gate. Now go half left through middle of field to stile (rather hidden) in top corner to enter hedged path – Love Walk.

Descending short flight of brick steps to reach road (Church Hill), with care cross over then turn left along footway to soon pass inside churchyard wall on right and to visit the attractive flint-faced part Norman Parish Church of St. Mary the Virgin. On leaving churchyard, note old village stocks on verge on left and on right, the old tithe barn converted to private residences. At road junction ahead, turn sharp right, along path through belt of trees and then turn right over stile into field on right, to follow hedge on left. At end of field at entrance to Sewage Works, turn left along concrete road for about 30 yards, then turn right along tarmac and gravel track through middle of large field. On reaching near corner of buildings (Heywood Farm) on left, turn right along winding track through fields which eventually enters woodland ahead up a gentle climb – Snowball Hill.

Just before M4 motorway bridge, turn sharp right over stile next to metal gate and follow field track curving left through corner of field. Immediately after gap in trees on right, bear right into path through narrow woodland strip and on emerging into field again, keep right along edge of field with ditch and hedge on right. In corner of field, turn left to continue up edge of field with fence of Waltham Place on right. At end of wodland, turn right over stile with adjacent footbridges, then continue along edge of two fields with woodland on right to reach stile next to wooden gate at road (B3024). With care turn right along road and at junction ahead, bear right along road (Church Hill), signposted 'Woodlands Park' – shortly note on right at edge of road, water fountain to commemorate sixty years of the reign of Queen Victoria.

About 20 yards before main entrance to Waltham Place on right, turn left up bank and over stile to follow edge of field with fence on left. Look ahead here for the spire of Shottesbrooke Church, and to right for distant view of Bowsey and Ashley Hills. At end of field turn right for about 20 yards before turning left over stile by gate. Follow hedge on right about half-way down field before bearing left to make for stile in far hedge, just to right of last power-line pole, next to houses. Keep along right-hand side of green (Walgrove Gardens) to road junction ahead, here cross over to pass behind Cricket Club pavilion and along edge of Cricket Ground. At path junction on far side of green, turn right towards War Memorial and continue along road ahead to shortly return to car park at start.

DATE WALKED | | 19

Help protect public paths and Common Land

Write to:

The Open Spaces Society, (Ref. EBRA)
25a Bell Street
Henley-on-Thames, Oxon RG9 2BA
Telephone: 0491 - 573535

Commons, Open Spaces & Footpaths
Preservation Society

Founded 1865

N

To Woodlands Park Ave.

Heywood Farm

To Maidenhead

Sewage Works

Snowball Hill

WHITE WALTHAM

To Knowl Hill

START HERE

Butchers Lane

Waltham Road

✝ St. Mary's

Love Walk

Waltham Place

Church Hill

Beehive P.H.

M4

Motorway

Paley Street Farm

B3024

To Holyport

To Twyford

0	¼	½ mile
0	¼	½ kilometre

Love Walk from Waltham Road.

Mire Lane and Crockford's Bridge

distance 4¹/₂ miles

This circular walk, of about 4¹/₂ miles in length, entirely in the Parish of Waltham St. Lawrence, is through the farmland and quiet lanes to the south of the village. In winter and after wet weather a few places can be muddy, so do go suitably shod.

The directions below start from Waltham St. Lawrence Parish Church (Grid Ref. 829769), but the map of the route may suggest other starting places or shorter alternatives. For further topographical features of the area, see the Ordnance Survey 1:25,000 'Pathfinder' series map Sheet 1173 'Windsor'. Please observe the Country Code.

With you back to the picturesque flint-faced part-11th century church of St. Lawrence, from The Pound turn right along road, then immediately bear left into Neville Close. At trees ahead, turn left through middle of field to a point on far boundary just to right of shed. Staying in same field, turn right and then left along edge of field with hedge on left to reach small wooden bridge with double stile. Now turn half-right through field ahead to stile in fence and in next field bear slightly left to reach in far left-hand corner, stile at bend in road, here with great care cross road (B3024) into gravel track opposite – Mire Lane.

About 50 yards after crossing concrete bridge over stream, turn left through field gateway and go ahead for about 30 yards to far boundary, then turn right to follow edge of field with trees and stream on left. After stile into second field, turn half-right to pass over footbridge with two stiles under large oak tree. Continue straight on through field ahead keeping parallel with hedge on right, to reach stile next to metal gate at road. Now turn right along road past the 'Plough' on right and after passing through left-hand bend, just before white cottage 'Dovercote' on right, turn left over stile and along edge of two fields with wooden fence on left. After far stile, enter woodland path and immediately before reaching field ahead turn left for about 10 yards, then turn

right over wooden footbridge. Go slightly right through middle of field to right-hand end of trees ahead, here after stile and footbridge and a further footbridge in about 50 yards, continue along edge of copse with ditch on left to reach road.

Turn left along road (Hungerford Lane) for about 80 yards, then turn left over stile next to metal gate and through middle of field to another stile at near end of hedgerow running down from distant house 'Goosenest'. Enter hedged path ahead, pass to left of 'Goosenest' and follow gravel track to road ahead, Baileys Lane, here turn right. Shortly at road junction, turn right into (Brook Lane) and immediately after last bungalow 'Brook Place' on left turn left into hedged track – Uncle's Lane. Follow this bridleway for about half-a-mile to eventually reach road, here turn left for just over 100 yards to reach – Crockford's Bridge.

Immediately after bridge take two right-hand turns and after about 30 yards along road, turn left into hedged track – Downfield Lane. Follow this track for nearly half-a-mile and at cross-roads of paths, turn left through concrete posts into path between high wire mesh fences to footbridge and stile at end. Keep straight on in field ahead, parallel with hedge on right, to another footbridge and stile. In next field follow edge of field with hedge on right, pass over stile to right of caravan site and continue ahead along Pool Lane to junction. With care turn right along road (B3024) keeping to verge for just over 100 yards and at junction turn left along road (Halls Lane). Immediately after cottages on right, turn left over stile next to metal gate and follow edge of field with hedge on right, then when hedge bends right, fork left through middle of field to stile in middle of far boundary hedge. Maintain same direction over stiles across corners of next two fields, then bear right along grass path with fence and trees on left and allotments on right. Pass through wooden swing gate ahead and turn right along road to return to start.

Ramble No. 15

DATE WALKED [　　] [19]

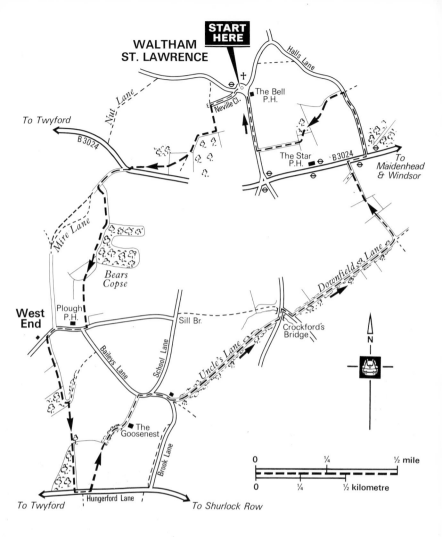

START
HERE

WALTHAM
ST. LAWRENCE

Halls Lane

The Bell
P.H.

Nut Lane

Neville Cl.

To Twyford

B 3024

The Star
P.H.   B3024

To
Maidenhead
& Windsor

Mire Lane

Bears
Copse

Downfield Lane

N

West
End

Plough
P.H.

Sill Br.

Crockford's
Bridge

Bailers Lane

School Lane

Uncle's Lane

The
Goosenest

Brook Lane

0   ¼   ½ mile

0   ¼   ½ kilometre

To Twyford   Hungerford Lane   To Shurlock Row

School Road – on the way via Sill Bridge

Around Ashley Hill

This circular walk, of about 3¹/₂ miles in length, uses several of the lesser-known footpaths around and over Ashley Hill, and at times provides some extensive views over the surrounding countryside.

The directions below start from the top of Dellars Hill, at bend in Honey Lane, near Burchetts Green (Grid Ref. 830813), by the entrance to Ashley Hill Woods (part of the Forestry Commission's Bramshill Forest), but the map of the route may suggest other starting places. For several years there was a parking area at the start, an amenity the Ramblers' Association would like to see restored.

For further topographical features of the area, see the Ordnance Survey 1:25,000 'Pathfinder' series map Sheet 1157 'Maidenhead and Marlow'. Please observe the Country Code. The waymarking (painted white arrows) to be seen on this walk, has been done by local members of the Ramblers' Association.

With your back to lane, walk up tarmac track for 50 yards to enter the 300 acre Ashley Hill Woods by stileway to side of gate. Follow climbing track to far end of broad ride on left, here turn left between posts into attractive gently descending woodland path. After small wooden footbridge over gulley, pass through stileway (opposite underground Ashley Hill Reservoir) and turn left down woodland track. Shortly cross over gravelled forest ride and continue straight on along woodland path. On reaching gravel ride again, cross over this and continue ahead on long straight gently descending broad woodland path. At end of path, pass through stileway, and continue for some 35 yards before turning right for about 150 yards along strip of common land parallel to busy Bath Road (A4).

Now bear right along gravel track – the large field to be seen on left is Bottle Meadow, the site used annually since 1971 for the Knowl Hill Steam Rally. After passing between red brick 'Kiln Cottage'

on left and the large pond on right, continue ahead through yard, bearing left to cross stile into first field on right. Pass to left of trees and follow fence soon on right to far end of field. At end of cattle pen go through squeeze-way and turn left along concrete track to reach road (Warren Row Road) beyond second gate. With care turn right along road for about 85 yards, then turn right again on to common land to follow winding waymarked woodland path.

On reaching path junction, turn left downhill for about 45 yards to property 'The Warren', then turn sharp right over stile next to wooden gate and keeping to higher part of two small fields make for stile under trees ahead. Climb up through middle of next field to another stile, then turn right to immediately pass over another stile next to metal gate and to follow firm fenced farm track – here look left for distant views of Warren Row and Pudders Farm. After stile at end of track continue along edge of field with fence on left, then after further stile and sloping footbridge turn left along track. In about 20 yards, pass through stileway and after another 20 yards cross stile and turn sharp right to follow edge of field with houses and fence on right to reach a further stile. Continue for about half-way down right-hand edge of next field, then turn right over sleeper footbridge with two stiles and immediately turn right again through wooden swing gate into broad hedged path to shortly pass 'The Dewdrop Inn' on left.

At top of rise ahead, turn left along narrow tarmac road to reach bend in road (Honey Lane), here turn right, before letter box, through stileway to climb steep woodland path – to avoid climb, turn left at stileway along the level but often wetter forest ride which runs parallel to Honey Lane. Near top of climb, keep straight on over forest ride and on reaching tarmac track turn left down hill to return to the start.

DATE WALKED   19

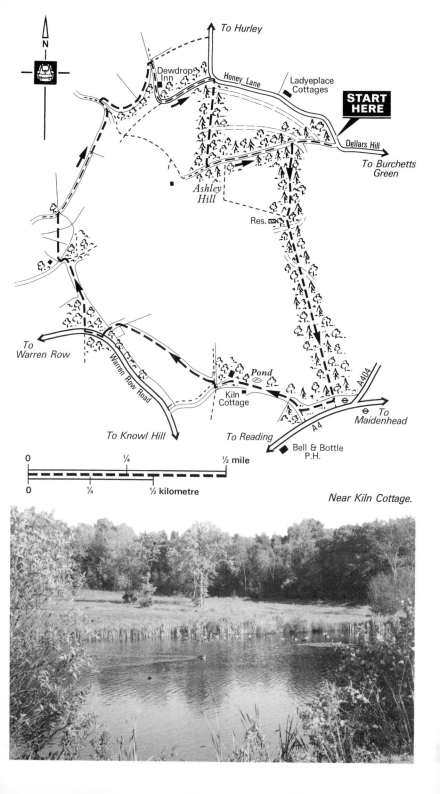

N

To Hurley

Dewdrop
Inn

Honey Lane

Ladyeplace
Cottages

**START
HERE**

Dellars Hill

To Burchetts
Green

*Ashley
Hill*

Res.

To
Warren Row

Warren Row Road

Pond

Kiln
Cottage

A404

To
Maidenhead

To Knowl Hill

To Reading

A4

Bell & Bottle
P.H.

0		¼		½ mile

0	¼	½ kilometre

Near Kiln Cottage.

Berghers Hill and Wooburn Green

distance 3 miles

This circular walk, of about 3 miles in length, climbs up to the woodlands around Berghers Hill and then descends to Wooburn Green before finally following the River Wye through Wooburn Park.

The directions below start from the car park in Wooburn Park (behind St. Paul's Church) at the foot of Wash Hill (Grid Ref. 910878), but the map of the route may suggest other starting places or shorter alternatives. For further topographical features of the area see the Ordnance Survey 1:25,000 'Pathfinder' series map Sheet 1157 'Maidenhead and Marlow'. Please observe the Country Code; in particular, keep to the footpaths, keep dogs on lead across farmland and leave all wild flowers for others to enjoy.

With your back to car park entrance, turn left up winding lane (Wash Hill). Towards top of hill, 20 yards after cul-de-sac Wash Hill Lea, turn right up bank to follow narrow wooded path between wire fence on right and road below on left. After stile, keep straight on up diagonal path through middle of field to middle of trees along top boundary of field, here enter copse ahead and bearing right, follow waymarked (painted white arrows) woodland path. Emerging from copse, follow well-defined path through middle of next field to road by 'The Chequers Inn', here turn left along road.

Follow this road for about half-a-mile through Widmoor, keeping to verges where possible, ignoring two turnings on right and keeping straight on at crossroads. On reaching forestry area (the Forestry Commission's Farm Wood) on left, turn left through wooden swing gate. Ignoring path on right, go straight ahead on gravel track - a permitted path - then just before BBC metal tower, bear left along woodland path, with field close on left. At corner of wood turn right and continue straight ahead, ignoring path on left at bottom of short steep decline. At top of short steep climb, at path junction, keep straight on along broad woodland path, then on reaching path junction at

facing fence, turn right up broad path to stile at – Berghers Hill.

Continue along short gravel path ahead between houses to reach tarmac road, here turn left along road and shortly enter fenced path to right of 'Coachman's Cottage'. On eventually reaching road junction at top of Windsor Hill, cross road into woodland opposite and immediately turn left down edge of wood with road nearby below on left. Emerging from woodland continue with hedge and road on left, then about three-quarters of way down field, pass over stile on left to descend to road by concrete steps. With care turn right down road and over the River Wye to eventually reach – Wooburn Green.

Now turn left along The Green passing the 'Queen & Albert' on left and War Memorial on right, then continue along Town Lane (A4094). At second estate road on left, turn left into Wooburn Manor Park. Where road bends right, bear left, in front of No 49, and shortly turn left to follow cul-de-sac, passing No 59. Immediately after bridge over River Wye, turn right and pass through gap in fence into Wooburn Park to follow river on right. When river turns right, keep straight ahead across open grass area in direction of church to return to car park at the start.

DATE WALKED   19

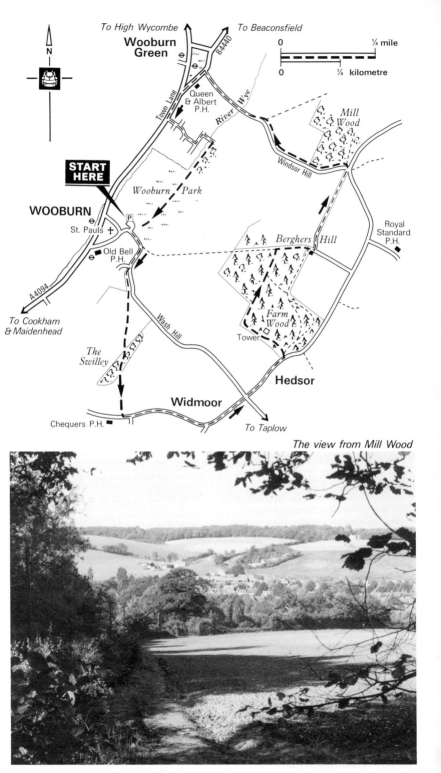

To High Wycombe
To Beaconsfield

Wooburn Green

B4440

N

Town Lane

Queen & Albert P.H.

River Wye

Mill Wood

Windsor Hill

START HERE

WOOBURN

Wooburn Park

P

St. Pauls

Old Bell P.H.

Berghers Hill

Royal Standard P.H.

A4094

To Cookham & Maidenhead

Wash Hill

Farm Wood

Tower

The Swilley

Hedsor

Widmoor

Chequers P.H.

To Taplow

0 ¼ mile

0 ¼ kilometre

The view from Mill Wood

Medmenham and Danesfield

distance 5 miles

This circular walk, of about 5 miles in length, visits the picturesque village of Medmenham (claimed to be the only riverside village in Buckinghamshire) and then passes through some fine beach woods north of Danesfield. The descent to the Thames at Hurley weir, has the fascination of passing through a 75 yard long tunnel (which does have two roof lights, but you may wish to carry a torch) – constructed by the Lord of the Manor as apparently he didn't like the general public walking across his front lawn.

The directions below start from the south end of Ferry Lane, Medmenham (Grid Ref. 806838) – here to the right, about 20 yards along the towpath, is the monument to commemorate the successful court action by Viscount Devonport in 1899 which decided that Medmenham Ferry was public – and to the left, hidden by the tall brick wall, is Medmenham Abbey, once the site of a 13th century Cistercian Abbey, rebuilt about 1745, it is perhaps better known for the notoriety of The Hell Fire Club founded by Sir Francis Dashwood. For further topographical features of the area, see the Ordnance Survey 1:25,000 'Pathfinder' series map Sheet 1157 'Maidenhead and Marlow'. Please observe the Country Code.

With your back to the river, follow Ferry Lane through village to the 12th century St. Peter's Church and the 16th century 'Dog and Badger' at road junction. With great care cross main road (A4155) into Bockmer Lane opposite, here after only 20 yards, look left into garden of 17th century cottage 'Gillmans' for a well preserved village pump and then look right, for start of the path up side of 1700 B.C. Contour Fort. After steep climb up waymarked (painted white arrows) path, bear right diagonally across top of fort through trees to reach metal swing gate, here turn left along gravel track, soon cross tarmac drive and pass through another metal swing gate to reach road ahead, at white house adjacent to 'The Old School'.

Now turn right to follow road and then gravel track. On approaching entrance to property 'The Hermitage' bear left to enter and descend stony fenced path. At 'Pheasantry Cottage' descend steeply on tarmac drive and after passing through entrance gate, turn right along drive. 60 yards beyond end of field on left, turn sharp left up narrow woodland path. Keep straight on along edge of wood soon with field below on left. About 85 yards after stile, immediately before metal swing gate, turn right steeply up hill past large white house on right to tarmac road, here turn left to soon enter gravel track with long flint wall to Danesfield Gardens on right. Continue through right-hand bend and at top of rise, bear left through concrete posts into woodland path with wire fence on right.

Keep straight on along well-defined waymarked path with houses at first on right and ignoring right fork at large clearing, continue ahead through woodland to eventually emerge just below road junction. Here turn right up road for about 50 yards, then turn right again into waymarked woodland path, keeping edge of wood nearby on left. Shortly the path bears right to join and follow woodland track. On reaching corner of field on left, bear slightly right to take right-hand fork in paths, crossing over to the other side of low earth bank. Continue ahead, soon to pass through an area of conifers and on reaching crossing path, about 80 yards before double wire mesh gates ahead, turn left and shortly right to cross earth bank again.

Now follow edge of woodland with housing estate nearby on right and then school playing field close on right. Cross stile at end of field and turn right to follow school boundary fence to reach stile at main road (A4155). With care turn right along road for about 275 yards, keeping to verge on right, then turn left across road to stile and through middle of field. At metal swing gate cross tarmac drive and about 60 yards ahead, enter

continued on next page

path with flint wall on left and metal railings on right. Shortly enter tunnel below Danesfield (once the home of R.A.F. Medmenham and now an hotel) and then descend steeply to reach River Thames at Hurley weir, here bear right along fenced path set back from river on left. Note at waters edge about 25 yards after crossing concrete bridge, the remnants of what is believed to be the last remaining winch used on the early 'flash' locks.

On reaching riverside house (Kingfishers Lodge, previously the Waterkeeper's Cottage) bear right, away from river along tarmac access road past Danesfield (Thames) Club on left, to eventually meet main road (A4155) at 'Medmenham' sign. With care turn left along verge for only a few yards before turning left into drive-way of Abbey Lodge. When level with house turn right through metal swing gate to soon reach stile. Now bear left through middle of field towards left-hand end of distant wooden buildings. Cross stile and follow path in same direction to reach footbridge and stile in corner of field. Follow woodland path and gravel drive, with stream on right, to road ahead. Here turn left to return to start.

The Danesfield Tunnel.

DATE WALKED ☐☐ 19

Penny's Lane and High Knowl Wood

This circular walk, of about 4 miles in length, is a rather hilly but scenic route through fields, lanes and woodlands around Crazies Hill, north of Wargrave. In winter and after wet weather, a few places on this walk can be rather muddy, so do go suitably shod. The waymarking (painted white arrows) is the work of local members of the Ramblers' Association.

The directions below start from Crazies Hill C.E. Primary School at the north end of Crazies Hill Road (Grid Ref. 799808), but the map of the route may suggest other starting places or shorter alternatives. For further topographical features of the area, see all four Ordnance Survey 1:25,000 'Pathfinder' series maps Sheets 1172 'Reading', 1156 'Henley-on-Thames', 1173 'Windsor' and 1157 'Maidenhead and Marlow'. Please observe the Country Code; in particular, keep to footpaths, keep dogs on lead across farmland and leave all wild flowers for others to enjoy.

With school entrance on your right, walk along road for nearly 100 yards and turn right into short hedged path immediately before large white property 'Summerfield House' – formerly Henley Town Hall, it was dismantled and reconstructed on this site at end of last century, to make way for a new building in the town to commemorate Queen Victoria's Jubilee. After stile, follow edge of field with fence on left and when fence bears left, keep straight on through middle of two fields in direction of distant communications tower, to reach stile at road (Worley's Lane) at left-hand end of six mature trees. Now turn left along road, pass buildings of Worley Farm on left and on reaching road junction at bottom of hill, turn left up bank and through metal swing gate to follow narrow path, enclosed between wire fences, which climbs up and over the hill, descending to stile at bottom of valley. Here turn left along sunken stony track - Penny's Lane.

Follow this slowly climbing track (with its right-hand bend) for about half-a-mile to eventually reach road, here turn right along road for about 30 yards, then turn left over sleeper footbridge. Keep along left-hand edge of garden to bungalow 'Penny Green' to enter field by stile and to follow edge of field with ditch and woodland on left. After next stile, continue ahead along grassy strip, through mature trees, to a further stile next to metal gate. At bottom of short descent turn left along field track towards buildings of Highlands Farm , to reach stile in left-hand corner of field, opposite farmhouse.

With care turn right along road for about 100 yards, then turn left over stile next to metal gate and go half-right up through middle of field to stile at path junction in top corner. Keep straight ahead on woodland path with fields nearby on right. Path descends, over wooden walk-way and across two gulleys to reach stile at edge of wood. Turn left along field edge, with woodland on left and at field corner pass to right of metal rails. For a short way follow stony stream bed, then continue on slowly climbing fenced path with Endalls Farm in distance on right and 'leg of mutton' field on left. After stile near top of climb, keep straight on into woodland and after further stile (near sawmill) turn left on descending path to enter woodland ahead. Now follow way-marked path, to eventually reach steep dip. Take path bearing right, up from this depression, to reach junction of five paths - High Knowl Wood.

Here go straight across junction for a few yards, before bearing right into woodland, not along grass track but along way-marked woodland path which runs parallel and to left of track. Eventually where path merges with track and track bends left, fork right down slope to reach stile next to gate at road. With care turn right along road (Highfield Road) and about 15 yards after entrance to first property 'The Paddocks' on right, turn left over stile into fenced and hedged path to emerge by stile and hedged path at the Village Hall at Crazies Hill, here turn right to return to start.

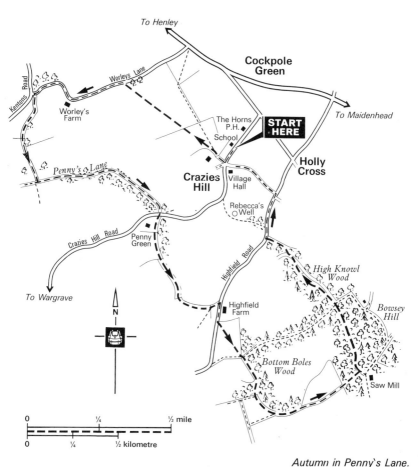

To Henley

Cockpole Green

Kentons Road

Worleys Lane

Worley's Farm

Penny's Lane

To Maidenhead

The Horns P.H.

School

START HERE

Holly Cross

Crazies Hill

Village Hall

Rebecca's Well

Penny Green

Crazies Hill Road

To Wargrave

Highfield Road

Highfield Farm

High Knowl Wood

Bowsey Hill

Bottom Boles Wood

Saw Mill

N

| 0 | ¼ | ½ mile |

| 0 | ¼ | ½ kilometre |

Autumn in Penny's Lane.

Lambridge Woods and Hernes Valley

distance 5 miles

This circular walk, of nearly 5 miles in length, after climbing out of Henley-on-Thames, crosses the golf course at Badgemore before entering Lambridge Woods – then after a glimpse of Grim's Ditch, the walk returns across farmland near Rotherfield Greys before descending to follow the bottom of the scenic Hernes Valley.

The directions below start from the car park in Kings Road, Henley-on-Thames (Grid Ref. 759828). For further topographical features of the area, see the Ordnance Survey 1:25,000 'Pathfinder' series map Sheet 1156 'Henley-on-Thames'. Please observe the Country Code; in particular, keep to footpaths, keep dogs on lead across farmland and leave all wild flowers for others to enjoy.

Leave car park by north exit (past modern library) and immediately cross over Kings Road into Mount View opposite. Follow this road through right-hand bend, then turn left up road with Mount View Court (Nos 19-32) on left. At end of road climb concrete steps and turn right along road, Hop Gardens, then at road junction turn left along Crisp Road. Immediately after property No. 71, turn left into fenced path and then right to climb up through field with fence nearby on left. At top of field, pass through metal swing gate and turn right along road (Lambridge Lane) - along here look right for views over Henley and Thames Valley. Keep straight on past two gateways with stiles and where tarmac drive finally turns right, cross stile to enter Badgemore Golf Course. Follow track through course, with strip of mature trees on left. At end of trees, with care bear slightly right across grass to enter woodland ahead - Lambridge Woods.

Continue straight on through woodland, keeping fence nearby on left, then after about 600 yards, (nearly 100 yards after climbing up from bottom of hollow adjacent to Grim's Ditch) turn left over stile and keep along edge of two fields with trees and then fence on right. At end of second field after stile next to field gate, with care cross road and turn right along verge for nearly 100 yards, then turn left over stile to follow concrete farm road (leading to New Farm) along edge of field. When farm road turns left, continue straight on along stony track with fence on left. Immediately after pit on left, turn left over fence to follow edge of field with fence and trees on right. At end of these trees, look half-right to village of Rotherfield Greys half-a-mile away on the horizon — to visit the 'Maltsters Arms' and 13th century St. Nicholas Church there, descend to bottom of field and take diagonal path (see map) along edge of field up side of valley. To continue walk, turn left at bottom of field and with fence and hedge on right, now follow the - Hernes Valley.

After stile in corner of field, keep straight on along field track in valley bottom, passing over two stiles below the attractive brick and timber house 'Lower Hernes' on left. Approaching end of valley pass over two stiles astride Pack and Prime Lane – a lane regularly used in the days when goods were brought up the Thames by barge – packhorses were loaded in Henley and taken by this route to Goring to avoid the long loop in the river. Keep straight on between fences with the playing fields of The Henley College on left to eventually reach metal swing gate, here continue ahead past cottages on left along gravel track with gardens to houses on right. Continue on tarmac drive and at road junction ahead, turn left along Paradise Road, then shortly at main road ahead, opposite entrance to Friar Park (home of Beatle George Harrison), with care cross over and turn right. Now fork left into West Street and at cross-roads, just after 'The Row Barge', turn left along Kings Road to return to car park at start.

DATE WALKED | | 19 |